I0163165

Dancing Off Country

By Thomas Jacob
Illustrated by Riker Matters

Library For All Ltd.

I was about ten when my grandfather first started teaching me and my brother how to do shake-a-leg.

He would take us to the school and teach us on the oval when it was empty.

We learned other dances too, some animal dances like the wallaby, and hunting dances.

I was so excited.

Learning the dances of my culture and bonding with my Elders made me happy.

I was even happier when I was chosen to dance at festivals and travel to perform.

We got to share our dances on other Countries with other mobs, showing them our culture and being shown theirs in return.

But it had been scary, travelling off Country to dance in front of people. I was both excited to perform and worried I would dance wrong.

Travelling to dance was also the first time I'd ever seen the city and Sydney Harbour! I've never been to the city before and I couldn't believe how high the buildings went!

There were so many people there. All the colours, lights and noises were a little overwhelming at first. But it was very exciting to see how other mob live and their Country.

13

I came back home from dancing on other Countries and decided to teach the young ones how to dance, too. My grandfather had been a good teacher, so I decided to teach just like him.

I wanted to be a role model for the young ones, like my grandfather had been for me. So, I took them to the oval and taught them shake-a-leg, the wallaby dance, and the hunter's dance.

18

I'll never forget travelling and dancing. I went from Brisbane to the far south of Tasmania. I wanted the young ones to experience that joy as well.

Our culture is strong and alive in my Country, and our dancing tells those stories. Now our young ones can tell those stories for a long time to come.

You can use these questions to talk about this book with your family, friends and teachers.

What did you learn from this book?

Describe this book in one word.
Funny? Scary? Colourful? Interesting?

How did this book make you feel when you finished reading it?

What was your favourite part of this book?

Download the Library For All Reader app from libraryforall.org

About the contributors

Thomas Jacobs was born on Thursday Island, Torres Strait Islands, but grew up on Mornington Island, Queensland. He is from the Lardil, Borroloda, Waanyi, and Bwgcolman mobs and loves dancing with his family and friends. His favourite stories as a child were the ones his grandfather told him about their culture.

Riker is a Noongar artist from Perth, Western Australia, with extensive experience in acrylic painting, digital art, illustration and design. Inspiration comes to Riker in all forms; they draw from the Earth, the Ocean, and what connects them emotionally to Country and soul.

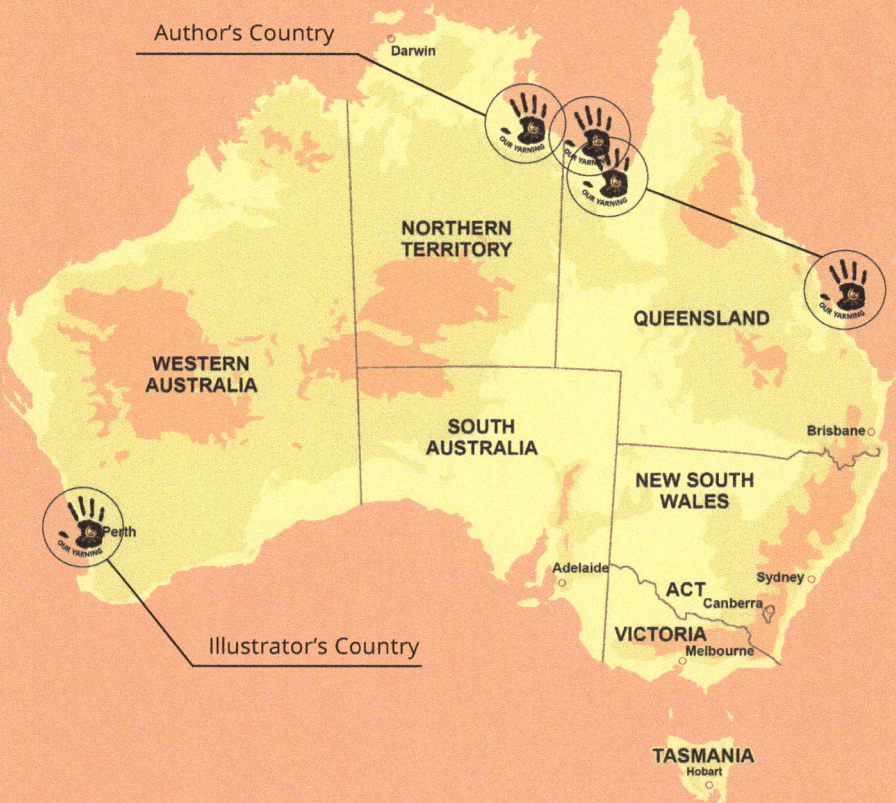

Author's Country

Darwin

NORTHERN
TERRITORY

QUEENSLAND

WESTERN
AUSTRALIA

SOUTH
AUSTRALIA

Brisbane

NEW SOUTH
WALES

Adelaide

Sydney

ACT
Canberra

VICTORIA
Melbourne

Perth

Illustrator's Country

TASMANIA
Hobart

Our Yarning

The Our Yarning collection aligns with the Australian Curriculum through the Cross-Curriculum Priorities — Aboriginal and Torres Strait Islander Histories and Cultures. The collection provides an authentic opportunity for learning and embedding Aboriginal and Torres Strait Islander perspectives because it is written by Aboriginal and Torres Strait Islander people.

We know that children learn better, and enjoy reading more, when they see themselves in the stories, characters and illustrations of the books they read.

To download the app, visit the Google Play Store or Apple Store and search 'Our Yarning'.

librarforall.org

You're reading Level 3

Learner – Beginner readers

Start your reading journey with short words, big ideas and plenty of pictures.

Level 1 – Rising readers

Raise your reading level with more words, simple sentences and exciting images.

Level 2 – Eager readers

Enjoy your reading time with familiar words, but complex sentences.

Level 3 – Progressing readers

Develop your reading skills with creative stories and some challenging vocabulary.

Level 4 – Fluent readers

Step up your reading skills with playful narratives, new words and fun facts.

Middle Primary – Curious readers

Discover your world through science and stories.

Upper Primary – Adventurous readers

Explore your world through science and stories.

Dancing Off Country

First published 2025

Published by Library For All Ltd
Email: info@libraryforall.org
URL: libraryforall.org

Our Yarning logo design by Jason Lee, Bidjipidji Art

Original illustrations by Riker Matters

Dancing Off Country
Jacob, Thomas
ISBN: 978-1-923485-65-5
SKU04847